Contents

How to Use This Book

The goal of *Measurement* is to increase learners' proficiency in mathematics skills at the kindergarten level. The subject matter featured in these activities has been chosen based on curriculum used in schools nationwide. The activities and skills follow a sampling of the National Council for the Teachers of Mathematics (NCTM) standards with a focus on science and social studies topics. These activities have been designed to capture learners' interests by presenting material in a fun and exciting way.

Measurement is organized into six sections: Size, Amount, Length, Weight, Volume, and Time. Each section focuses on an important aspect of measurement, offering easy-to-understand skill definitions and activity directions.

Size

In this section, learners practice visually identifying which object is larger or smaller in a pair of objects, as well as distinguishing the largest and smallest objects in a collection of three objects.

Amount

Activities that focus on counting a given number of objects are featured in this section. Learners are also taught to compare two groups of objects and determine which one has more and which has less.

2

Length

Learners are encouraged to compare different measurements of length in this section, focusing specifically on the concepts of taller and shorter, longer and shorter, and nearer and farther. Learners are also introduced to measuring length using nonstandard units.

Weight

This section features activities that require learners to compare weights of two or three objects in a group and determine which is heavier or lighter, or which is heaviest or lightest. Learners also receive instruction on how to use a balance scale.

Volume

In this section, learners compare groups of two or three containers and determine which one holds more or less, or which hold most or least.

Time

Telling time by the hour is the highlighted skill in this section. Learners practice matching times shown on a clock with written times. They also practice how to write the time shown on a clock in two different ways.

Name _____

Which Is Larger?

When we compare 2 objects of different sizes, 1 object is larger.

Directions: In each row, put an X on the shape that is larger.

1.

2.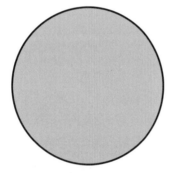

3.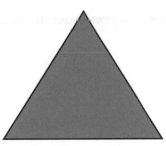

© Rosen School Supply•Brain Builders Measurement•K•RSS

Name _____

Which Has More?

We can count the number of objects in a group.

Directions: We like to play sports. In each row, count the number of balls in each group. Circle the group that has more.

1.

2.

3.

Name _____

Which Is Longer?

We can compare 2 objects to see which is longer.

Directions: Grasshoppers are insects that can jump! Look at each row. Circle the grasshopper that is longer.

1.

2.

3.

Name _____

Which Is Heavier?

We can compare 2 objects to see which is heavier.

Directions: Turtles are animals with shells. Some turtles are big and heavy. Some turtles are small and light. In each row, circle the turtle that is heavier.

1.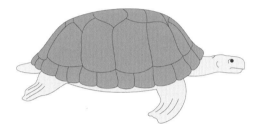

2.

3.

7

Name _____

Which Holds More?

We can compare 2 containers to see which holds more.

> ✏ **Directions: We use different containers every day. In each row, circle the container that holds more.**

1.

2.

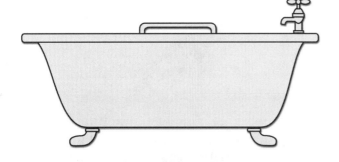

3.

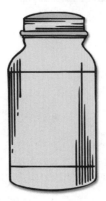 

Name _____

What Time Is It?

We can look at a clock to see what time it is.

✏️ **Directions: Circle the clock in each row that shows the time in the box.**

1. | 2:00 |

2. | 8:00 |

3. | 11:00 |

Background

- Learners benefit from practice and repetition with basic measurement concepts. Comparing the sizes of familiar objects in sports, nature, transportation, and the community helps them to understand the concepts of larger, smaller, largest, and smallest.

Homework Helper

- Collect a number of different-sized items found in the home. Find 2 objects that have obvious size differences and ask the learner to identify which object is larger and which is smaller. Repeat this process several times with different sets of objects. Next, display groups of 3 different-sized objects. Encourage learners to identify the largest and smallest items in each group.

Research-based Activity

- Show learners how to use educational software that reinforces the following concepts related to size: larger, smaller, largest, smallest. Ask parent volunteers and older students to instruct early learners on the basics of computer use and to provide help as needed.

Test Prep

- Learners at this level are introduced to activities that will prepare them for the testing format they will encounter on standardized tests beginning in higher elementary grades. The test preparation skills covered in this section include reading and following directions, and selecting answers from a multiple-choice format.

Different Audiences

- To adapt this section to an ESL learner, show them pairs of pictures depicting a large object and a small object. Have them first identify the object as large or small in their native language, then in English.

Name _____

Let's Play Sports!

When we compare 2 objects of different sizes, 1 object is larger than the other object.

Directions: Sports are fun! We need a ball to play some sports. Look at the balls in each row. Color the ball that is larger.

1.

2.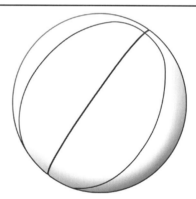

3.

FUN FACT

Have you ever played softball?
Softball is a lot like baseball!

Name _____

So Many Bugs

When we compare 2 objects of different sizes, 1 object is smaller than the other object.

Directions: You can find bugs almost everywhere—in your house, in your backyard, at the park, and underwater! Look at the bugs in each row below. Circle the bug that is smaller.

1.

2.

3.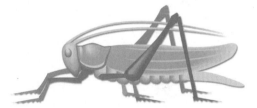

 A honeybee can beat its wings about 250 times a second!

Name _____

How We Get Around

When we compare 3 objects of different sizes, 1 object is the largest.

Directions: A car is large. A truck is larger. An airplane is largest! These things all help us get where we need to go. Look at the 3 objects in each row below. Circle the one that is largest.

1.

_____

2.

 Some jet planes are so big they are called "jumbo jets."

13

Name _____

People in My Community

When we compare 3 objects of different sizes, 1 object is the smallest.

Directions: People in our community use different things to do their jobs. Read each example. Look at the 3 objects. Circle the one that is smallest.

1. A police officer uses these things.

2. A teacher uses these things.

FUN FACT

Police officers sometimes use dogs to help them do their jobs.

Name _____

Skill Check—Size

Directions: Circle the one that is larger.

Directions: Color the one that is smaller.

Directions: Circle the one that is largest.

Directions: Circle the one that is smallest.

Teaching Tips...

Background

- Counting and comparing groups of objects is an important skill for early learners. Understanding more and less helps learners describe different quantities and prepares them for higher-level math skills.

Homework Helper

- Separate familiar objects into 2 unequal sets. Provide cards numbered 1–10. Ask the learner to count the items in each set and place the correct number card under each one, then have them identify which group has more and which has less.

Research-based Activity

- With the help of a parent, have learners select photographs of family members or friends. Ask learners to count the number of people in each photograph, then tell which photograph shows the most people and which photograph shows the fewest people.

Test Prep

- Learners at this level are introduced to activities that will prepare them for the testing format they will encounter on standardized tests beginning in higher elementary grades. The test preparation skills covered in this section include reading and following directions, filling in the blank, and choosing the correct answer.

Different Audiences

- To adapt this section to an accelerated learner, provide the learner with a pair of pictures, each picture showing a different number of animals. Have the learner write 2 sentences that compare the amounts shown in each picture. (Example: There are more cats than dogs. There are less dogs than cats.)

TEACHING TIPS

16

Name _____

Baby Animals

We can count the number of objects in a group.

✏️ **Directions: All animals were once babies. Count the number of baby animals in each row. Write the number on the line.**

Example:

      <u>4</u>

1.    _____

2.      _____

FUN FACT   Baby elephants can be 3 feet tall when they are born!

Name _____

Map Math

The number of objects in 2 groups can be counted and compared.

Directions: We use maps to learn about places we live and places we go. This is a map of a small town. Use it to answer the questions below.

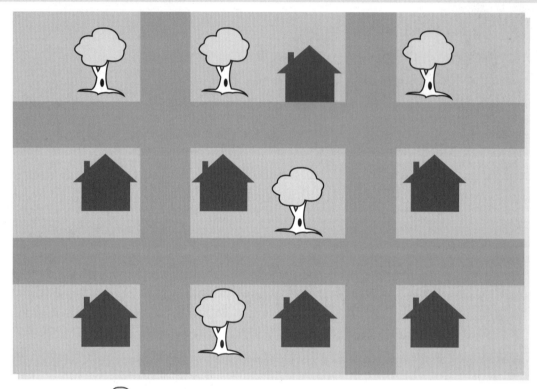

1. How many 🌳 do you see? _____

2. How many 🏠 do you see? _____

3. Are there more 🏠 or 🌳 ? _____

Maps of towns often show the names of streets, parks, and buildings.

Name _____

Families

When comparing 2 groups that have different numbers of objects,
1 group has more objects than the other.

Directions: Families are all different. Some families have many people in them. Some families have 2 or 3 people. Count the people in each family below. Circle the family in each row that has more people.

1.

2.

3.

FUN FACT Families can include grandparents, great-grandparents, aunts, uncles, and cousins.

19

Name _____

Seeds

*When comparing 2 groups that have different numbers of objects,
1 group has less objects than the other.*

Directions: Fruits and vegetables grow from seeds. Look at the groups of seeds in each row. Circle the group in each row that has less seeds.

1.

2.

3.

FUN FACT   Sunflowers have seeds
you can eat!

Name _____

Skill Check—Amount

Directions: Count how many are in each group. Write the number on the line.

_____   _____

Directions: Circle the group that has more.

Directions: Circle the group that has less.

Background

• At this level, instruction on length focuses on the concepts of longest and shortest. Learners also practice using nonstandard units of measurement to measure objects. The concepts of taller and shorter are used to describe height, and the concepts of near and far are used to describe relative distance.

Homework Helper

• Have learners use items such as pencils and blocks to measure the length of different objects in their home. (Example: My bed is as long as 20 pencils.) Ask learners to identify which object they measured was longest and which was shortest.

Research-based Activity

• With the help of a parent or older student, have learners look at a simple map of the place they live. Identify where the learners' school is on the map, then guide them in telling which places on the map are near their school and which are farther away.

Test Prep

• Learners at this level are introduced to activities that will prepare them for the testing format they will encounter on standardized tests beginning in higher elementary grades. The test preparation skills covered in this section include following directions, selecting the correct answer, and writing the correct answer.

Different Audiences

• To adapt this section to a special needs learner, provide sets with 2 familiar objects, such as a pencil and a crayon. Have the learner compare the lengths of the 2 objects and identify which is longer and which is shorter.

TEACHING TIPS

Name _____

Taller and Shorter

When we compare 2 objects of different heights, 1 object is taller and 1 object is shorter.

People look different in many ways. Some have dark hair and some have light hair. Some are tall and some are short. These differences make us special. In each example, circle the person who is taller. Put an X on the person who is shorter.

1.

2.

FUN FACT

The tallest man who ever lived was almost 9 feet tall!

23

Name _____

Lots of Snakes

When we compare 3 objects of different lengths, 1 object is the longest and 1 object is the shortest.

Directions: There are many kinds of snakes. Snakes come in many sizes. Look at the snakes below. In each row, circle the snake that is longest. Put an X on the snake that is shortest.

Example:

 X

1.

2.

The largest snake ever found was more than 32 feet long!

Name _____

Fish Are Fun!

We can use different things to measure the length of an object.

> ✏️ **Directions:** Fish are animals that live in water. They come in different colors and sizes. Look at each fish and the boxes below it. Count the number of boxes that are the same as the length of the fish. Write the number on the line.

Example:

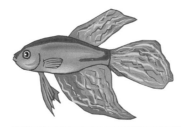

3

1.

_____

2.

_____

FUN FACT Most fish have fins that help them swim.

25

Name _____

Nearer or Farther?

We can use a map to find out which places are nearer and which places are farther away.

Directions: Look at the map. Jerry's house is near the middle of the map. Read each question. Circle the correct answer.

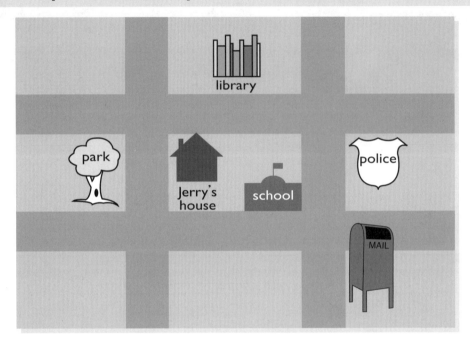

1. Which is nearer to Jerry's house?

2. Which is farther from Jerry's house?

You can use a map to find where places are in your city or town.

26

Name _____

Skill Check—Length

Directions: Circle the one that is longest. Put an X on the one that is shortest.

Directions: Circle the one that is tallest. Put a box around the one that is shortest.

Teaching Tips...

TEACHING TIPS

Background

• The ability to compare the weights of different objects relies on a basic understanding of the terms *heavy* and *light*. Learners can then identify the heavier or lighter object in a pair of objects, as well as the heaviest and lightest object in a group of 3 or more objects.

Homework Helper

• Give learners 2 sheets of paper, 1 labeled *Heavy* and 1 labeled *Light*. Tell them to look around their home for an object that is heavy and an object that is light, and to draw a picture of the item on the appropriate piece of paper.

Research-based Activity

• Provide a balance scale and familiar items of various weights for students to weigh. Assist learners with weighing their objects on the balance scale. Ask them to make up a statement that tells which object was heavier and which object was lighter.

Test Prep

• Learners at this level are introduced to activities that will prepare them for the testing format they will encounter on standardized tests beginning in higher elementary grades. The test preparation skills covered in this section include reading and following directions, and selecting the correct answer.

Different Audiences

• To adapt this section to an accelerated learner, ask the learner to look at a group of 3 objects or pictures in the same category and identify which one is the lightest and which one is the heaviest. Ask the learner to write 2 sentences comparing the objects in each group.

Name _____

Fun with Fruits

When we compare 2 objects of different weights, 1 object is heavier than the other.

Directions: We buy fruits at the store. We weigh them to find out how much they cost. Circle the fruit in each row that is heavier.

1.

2.

3.

FUN FACT   Apples grow on apple trees.

29

Name _____

Animals at the Zoo

When we compare 2 objects of different weights, 1 object is lighter than the other.

 Directions: There are many animals at the zoo. Some are big and heavy. Some are small and light. Look at the pairs of zoo animals in each row. Circle the animal that is lighter.

1.

2.

3.

FUN FACT

The smallest monkey in the world weighs less than 1 pound!

Name _____

Tools

When we compare 3 objects of different weights, 1 object is the heaviest and 1 object is the lightest.

Directions: We use tools to make a job easier. Look at the tools in each row. Circle the tool that is heaviest. Put an X on the tool that is lightest.

1.

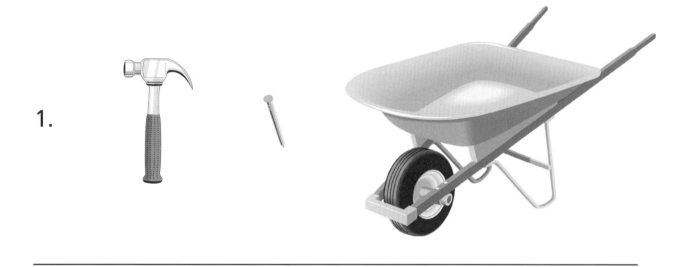

2.

FUN FACT

The first tools were made of sticks and rocks.

Name _____

Using a Scale

We can use a balance scale to compare the weights of 2 objects.

Directions: A balance scale is a special kind of scale. When we put 2 objects on a balance scale, the heavier object goes down and the lighter object goes up. Look at the balance scales below. On each scale, circle the object that is heavier.

1.

2.

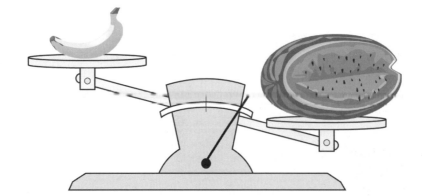

FUN FACT

If you weigh 2 things on a balance scale and neither thing goes up or down, both things weigh the same.

Name _____

Skill Check—Weight

✏️ **Directions:** In each example, circle the one that is heavier.

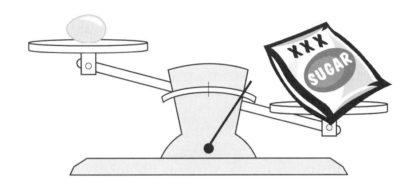

✏️ **Directions:** Circle the one that is lightest.

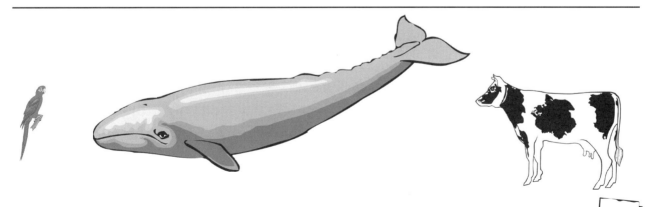

33

Teaching Tips...

Background

• Learners can best understand how to measure volume through activities that compare different-sized containers and teach them that different containers hold different amounts. Understanding this concept can help learners use this skill in everyday situations.

Homework Helper

• After completing the activities on pages 37 and 38, ask learners to have a parent help them find 3 containers from their home, such as a plastic cup, a plastic bowl, and a plastic milk carton. Have them tell which container holds the most and which container holds the least.

Research-based Activity

• Provide learners with flowerpots of different sizes, soil, and flower seeds. Assist them with research on the Internet or at the library to determine how many seeds and how much soil their flowerpot can hold, and how much water their plant will need to grow.

Test Prep

• Learners at this level are introduced to activities that will prepare them for the testing format they will encounter on standardized tests beginning in higher elementary grades. The test preparation skills covered in this section include reading and following directions and selecting the correct answer.

Different Audiences

• To adapt this section to an accelerated learner, show the learner 2 different-sized jars of jellybeans, one clearly holding more than the other. Have the learner identify which jar holds more and which holds less, then have them guess how many jellybeans are in each jar.

Name _____

It Holds More

When we compare 2 containers that hold different amounts,
1 container holds more than the other.

Directions: Look at the containers in each row. Circle the one that holds more.

1.

2.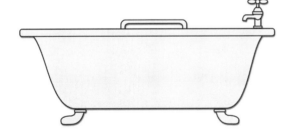

3.

A balloon is a kind of
container. It holds air!

Name _____

From the Farm to the Store

When we compare 2 containers that hold different amounts, 1 container holds less than the other.

 Directions: Farmers grow fruits and vegetables and send them to stores. People buy the fruits and vegetables to eat. In each row, circle the container that holds less.

1.

2.

3.

FUN FACT

Apples can be red, green, or yellow.

Name _____

Bottles and Cans

When comparing 3 containers that hold different amounts,
1 container holds the most.

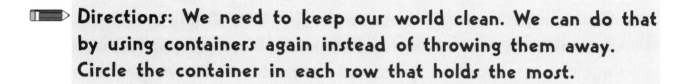 **Directions:** We need to keep our world clean. We can do that by using containers again instead of throwing them away. Circle the container in each row that holds the most.

1.

2.

3.

 **FUN FACT**

Milk comes in containers. Milk helps keep your bones strong.

37

Name _____

Let's Plant!

When comparing 3 containers that hold different amounts,
1 container holds the least.

Directions: Most plants grow in the dirt. Small plants need less dirt to grow. Large plants need more dirt to grow. In each row, circle the pot that holds the least amount of dirt.

1.

2.

FUN FACT

You can grow your own plant!

Name _____

Skill Check—Volume

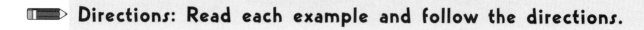

Directions: Read each example and follow the directions.

1. Circle the one that holds **more**.

2. Circle the one that holds **less**.

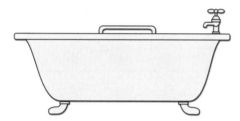

3. Circle the one that holds the **most**.

4. Circle the one that holds the **least**.

  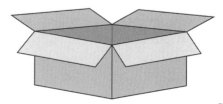

Teaching Tips...

Background

• The basics of telling time by the hour are introduced at this level. Learners will receive practice with reading and writing different ways to show the time—with numbers and with words.

Homework Helper

• Assist learners in setting up a "time diary" on a piece of paper with headings such as: *I wake up, I go to school, I eat lunch, I eat dinner, I go to bed*. Beneath each heading, ask learners to write the time they perform each activity.

Research-based Activity

• Have learners use the "time diary" concept to do research on a friend or family member's daily schedule. Have them draw pictures of some daily activities, then write the times their friend or family member performs those activities.

Test Prep

• Learners at this level are introduced to activities that will prepare them for the testing format they will encounter on standardized tests beginning in higher elementary grades. The test preparation skills covered in this section include following directions, matching pictures and labels, and writing the correct answers to questions.

Different Audiences

• To adapt this section to an ESL learner, provide the learner with a commercial or teacher-made clock. Show and say times by the hour in the learner's language, then in English. Ask the learner to arrange the hands on the clock to show the times and to repeat the time in English.

Name _____

What Time Is It?

We can look at a clock and write the time it shows using numbers.

> **Directions: Look at each clock below. Then write in the time it shows on the line.**

Example:

3:00

_____

1.

_____

2.

_____

3.

_____

 There are 60 minutes in 1 hour.

41

Name _____

Time to Match!

We can match the time shown on a clock with the written time.

> **Directions:** The clocks below show times by the hour. Draw a line from each clock to the correct written time.

Example:

9:00

1.

4:00

2.

11:00

3.

2:00

FUN FACT

The longer hand on a clock is the minute hand. The shorter hand is the hour hand.

Name _____

Telling Time

We can use a clock to tell time by the hour.

Directions: Read each question. Circle the clock that shows the correct answer.

1. Which clock shows 7:00?

2. Which clock shows 12:00?

3. Which clock shows 3:00?

FUN FACT

There are 24 hours in a day.

43

Name _____

Time to Write!

We can use words to show the time.

✎➤ **Directions:** On this clock, the hour hand is on the 9 and the minute hand is on the 12. This is written as 9:00 and as "nine o'clock." Look at each clock. Write the time in words on the line.

nine o'clock

Example:

three o'clock

1.

_____

2.

_____

FUN FACT

The word "o'clock" is short for "of the clock."

Name _____

Skill Check—Time

✏️➤ **Directions: Read each example and follow the directions.**

1. What time does this clock show? Write your answer using numbers.

_____

2. Circle the clock that shows 9:00.

3. What time does this clock show? Write your answer using words.

_____

Answer Key

p. 4
1. There should be an X on the second square.
2. There should be an X on the first circle.
3. There should be an X on the first triangle.

p. 5
1. The first group should be circled.
2. The first group should be circled.
3. The second group should be circled.

p. 6
1. The first grasshopper should be circled.
2. The second grasshopper should be circled.
3. The first grasshopper should be circled.

p. 7
1. The second turtle should be circled.
2. The first turtle should be circled.
3. The second turtle should be circled.

p. 8
1. The pitcher should be circled.
2. The bathtub should be circled.
3. The larger jar should be circled.

p. 9
1. The first clock should be circled.
2. The second clock should be circled.
3. The second clock should be circled.

p. 11
1. The first ball should be colored.
2. The second ball should be colored.
3. The first ball should be colored.

p. 12
1. The second bug should be circled.
2. The first bug should be circled.
3. The first bug should be circled.

p. 13
1. The boat should be circled.
2. The car should be circled.

p. 14
1. The whistle should be circled.
2. The book should be circled.

p. 15
The butterfly should be circled.
The tennis ball should be colored.
The middle turtle should be circled.
The middle dog should be circled.

p. 17
1. 2
2. 3

p. 18
1. 5
2. 7
3. There should be a picture of a house drawn.

p. 19
1. The first family should be circled.
2. The second family should be circled.
3. The first family should be circled.

p. 20
1. The first group should be circled.
2. The first group should be circled.
3. The second group should be circled.

p. 21
3, 4
The first group should be circled.
The picture of the girl should be circled.

p. 23
1. The man should be circled.
   There should be an X on the boy.
2. The woman should be circled.
   There should be an X on the boy.

p. 24
1. The third snake should be circled.
   There should be an X on the second snake.
2. The first snake should be circled.
   There should be an X on the third snake.

p. 25
1. 2
2. 4

p. 26
1. The school picture should be circled.
2. The mailbox picture should be circled.

p. 27
The second snake should be circled.
There should be an X on the first snake.
The man in the middle should be circled.
There should be a box drawn around the boy.

p. 29
1. The pineapple should be circled.
2. The melon should be circled.
3. The pumpkin should be circled.

p. 30
1. The monkey should be circled.
2. The parrot should be circled.
3. The snake should be circled.

p. 31
1. The wheelbarrow should be circled.
   There should be an X on the nail.
2. The large shovel should be circled.
   There should be an X on the screw.

p. 32
1. The large carton of milk should be circled.
2. The watermelon should be circled.

p. 33
The dog should be circled.
The bag of sugar should be circled.
The sneaker should be circled.
The parrot should be circled.

p. 35
1. The pitcher should be circled.
2. The bathtub should be circled.
3. The pool should be circled.

p. 36
1. The second picture
   should be circled.
2. The first picture
   should be circled.
3. The first picture
   should be circled.

p. 37
1. The second picture
   should be circled.
2. The third picture
   should be circled.
3. The first picture
   should be circled.

p. 38
1. The second pot should
   be circled.
2. The third pot should
   be circled.

p. 39
1. The pitcher should
   be circled.
2. The glass should
   be circled.
3. The second bowl
   should be circled.
4. The first box should
   be circled.

p. 41
1. 7:00
2. 6:00
3. 4:00

p. 42
1. There should be a line
   connecting the clock
   to 2:00.
2. There should be a line
   connecting the clock
   to 4:00.
3. There should be a line
   connecting the clock
   to 9:00.

p. 43
1. The first clock should
   be circled.
2. The first clock should
   be circled.
3. The second clock
   should be circled.

p. 44
1. ten o'clock
2. five o'clock

p. 45
1. 2:00
2. The first clock should
   be circled.
3. four o'clock